The Not So Fun Fair

PHASE 3
AND 4

/air/
ure/

Level 4 – Blue

BookLife

Helpful Hints for Reading at Home

The graphemes (written letters) and phonemes (units of sound) used throughout this series are aligned with Letters and Sounds. This offers a consistent approach to learning whether reading at home or in the classroom.

HERE IS A LIST OF NEW GRAPHEMES FOR THIS PHASE OF LEARNING. AN EXAMPLE OF THE PRONUNCIATION CAN BE FOUND IN BRACKETS.

Phase 3			
j (jug)	v (van)	w (wet)	x (fox)
y (yellow)	z (zoo)	zz (buzz)	qu (quick)
ch (chip)	sh (shop)	th (thin/then)	ng (ring)
ai (rain)	ee (feet)	igh (night)	oa (boat)
oo (boot/look)	ar (farm)	or (for)	ur (hurt)
ow (cow)	oi (coin)	ear (dear)	air (fair)
ure (sure)	er (corner)		

HERE ARE SOME WORDS WHICH YOUR CHILD MAY FIND TRICKY.

Phase 3 Tricky Words			
he	you	she	they
we	all	me	are
be	my	was	her

Phase 4 Tricky Words			
said	were	have	there
like	little	so	one
do	when	some	out
come	what		

GPC focus: /air/ure/

TOP TIPS FOR HELPING YOUR CHILD TO READ:

- Allow children time to break down unfamiliar words into units of sound and then encourage children to string these sounds together to create the word.

- Encourage your child to point out any focus phonics when they are used.

- Read through the book more than once to grow confidence.

- Ask simple questions about the text to assess understanding.

- Encourage children to use illustrations as prompts.

PHASE 3 AND 4

/air/ ure/

This book focuses on the phonemes /air/ and /ure/ and is a blue level 4 book band.

The Not So Fun Fair

Written by
Sophie Hibberd

Illustrated by
Marcus Gray

The children get off the bus. "Can you get into pairs?" asks Miss Reed.

Blair is in a pair with Jack. Being up in the air is fun for Jack, but Blair feels secure on the path.

"Let's go on that!" yells Jack. He points to a big red and green coaster.

Blair has a fear of being high up in the air. "I will stand back and wait for you."

"Are you sure you will not go on?" asks Miss Reed.

"I can assure you it is fun and secure."

"I am sure." Blair sits down on the stairs and waits.

"Can I go on Star Blast?" asks Jack.
"It is so high in the air!"

Star Blast has floating rockets that go up and down with gears. Blair feels sick and limp.

"Can I wait?" asks Blair.
"Are you sure you will not go on?" asks
Miss Reed.

"You have been waiting all year to come to the fair."

"I am sure, I have a fear of being up in the air."

Some of the children snicker. Blair feels tears well up, but she turns so they do not see.

There is a man yelling from a stand near Star Blast.

He is mature and has a long beard.

"Pop all three ping-pong balls into the cup and win a star coin!" yells the man.

Blair visits the stand. "Can I have a go?" asks Blair.

The man with the beard puts three
ping-pong balls into her hand.

"Get all three in and you will win a star coin that can grant a wish."

Blair chucks a ball and gets it in the cup.
The next ball lands in the cup too!

"One ball to go. I am sure you can do it!"

Blair lets the last ball go... it lands in the cup! "Yes, I did it!" yells Blair.

"Good job!" yells the man. Blair has the star coin in her hand.

"Let's go on the swinging chairs!" yells Jack.

"Shall I wait with you, Blair?" asks Miss Reed.

"No, Miss Reed, I will go on too!"

The Not So Fun Fair

1.   Who was Blair in a pair with?

     (a) Jill

     (b) Miss Reed

     (c) Jack

2.   What does Blair have a fear of?

3.   Can you explain how Star Blast works?

4.   How does Blair win a star coin?

5.   Why do you think Blair became brave enough to go on the swinging chairs? When have you shown bravery?

©2021 **BookLife Publishing Ltd.**
King's Lynn, Norfolk PE30 4LS

ISBN 978-1-83927-395-7

The Not So Fun Fair
Written by Sophie Hibberd
Illustrated by Marcus Gray

An Introduction to BookLife Readers...

Our Readers have been specifically created in line with the London Institute of Education's approach to book banding and are phonetically decodable and ordered to support each phase of Letters and Sounds.

Each book has been created to provide the best possible reading and learning experience. Our aim is to share our love of books with children, providing both emerging readers and prolific page-turners with beautiful books that are guaranteed to provoke interest and learning, regardless of ability.

BOOK BAND GRADED using the Institute of Education's approach to levelling.

PHONETICALLY DECODABLE supporting each phase of Letters and Sounds.

EXERCISES AND QUESTIONS to offer reinforcement and to ascertain comprehension.

BEAUTIFULLY ILLUSTRATED to inspire and provoke engagement, providing a variety of styles for the reader to enjoy whilst reading through the series.

AUTHOR INSIGHT:
SOPHIE HIBBERD

Inspired by a love of reading with a strong influence from characters like Matilda, Sophie always knew she would love to write. During her teen years Sophie explored the literary world by writing her very own novels and short stories. She then went on to self-publish these on an app where thousands have read them. Since then, Sophie went on to achieve an impressive 2:1 degree in English Literature and Creative Writing from Anglia Ruskin. Out of education, Sophie has been working for educational companies across Norfolk, and now is writing her very first set of children's books for BookLife Publishing.

PHASE 3 AND 4
/air/
/ure/

This book focuses on the phonemes /air/ and /ure/ and is a blue level 4 book band.